M000222627

The Hotel Eden

Beverley Bie Brahic is a poet, translator and occasional critic. Her collection *White Sheets* was a finalist for the 2012 Forward Prize; *Hunting the Boar* (2016) was a Poetry Book Society Recommendation, and her translation, *Guillaume Apollinaire, The Little Auto,* won the 2013 Scott Moncrieff Prize. Other translations include *Francis Ponge, Unfinished Ode to Mud,* a 2009 Popescu Prize finalist, and books by Hélène Cixous, Yves Bonnefoy, Jacques Derrida and Julia Kristeva. Brahic was born in Saskatoon, Canada, grew up in Vancouver, and now lives in Paris and the San Francisco Bay Area.

also by Beverley Bie Brahic

POETRY

Hunting the Boar
White Sheets
Against Gravity

SELECTED POETRY TRANSLATIONS

Unfinished Ode To Mud by Francis Ponge
The Little Auto by Guillaume Apollinaire
The Present Hour by Yves Bonnefoy
The Anchor's Long Chain by Yves Bonnefoy
Rue Traversière by Yves Bonnefoy
Ursa Major by Yves Bonnefoy

SELECTED PROSE TRANSLATIONS

Twists and Turns in the Heart's Antarctic by Hélène Cixous
Hemlock by Hélène Cixous
Hyperdream by Hélène Cixous
Manhattan by Hélène Cixous
Dream I Tell You by Hélène Cixous
The Day I Wasn't There by Hélène Cixous
Reveries of The Wild Woman by Hélène Cixous
Portrait of Jacques Derrida as a Young Jewish Saint by Hélène Cixous
Geneses, Genealogies, Genres and Genius by Jacques Derrida
This Incredible Need to Believe by Julia Kristeva

BEVERLEY BIE BRAHIC

The Hotel Eden

CARCANET

First published in Great Britain in 2018 by
Carcanet Press Ltd
Alliance House, 30 Cross Street
Manchester M2 7AQ
www.carcanet.co.uk

Text copyright © Beverley Bie Brahic, 2018

The right of Beverley Bie Brahic to be identified as the author of this work
has been asserted by her in accordance with the Copyright, Designs and
Patents Act of 1988.
All rights reserved.

A CIP catalogue record for this book is available from the British Library.
ISBN 978 1 784106 10 2

The publisher acknowledges financial assistance from Arts Council England.

Typeset in England by XL Publishing Services, Exmouth
Printed and bound in England by SRP Ltd, Exeter

Contents

Acknowledgements

Thanks are due to the editors of the following journals in which some of these poems first appeared, some in earlier versions: *American Journal of Poetry*, *The Hudson Review*, *Manchester Review*, *Mantis*, *Poetry Ireland Review*, *PN Review*, *Poetry Daily*, *Poetry Review*, *Queen's Quarterly*, *Recours au poème*, *Shofar*, *Stand* and *La Traductière*.

Indra's Net, an anthology published by Bennison Books in support of The Book Bus Charity, published an earlier version of 'The Sand Dollar Inn'.

'Letter Home' is adapted from Bill Rawling, *Death their Enemy: Canadian Medical Practitioners and War*.

I am grateful to my first readers for their spot-on criticisms and encouragement, especially Nina Bogin, in France, and Chana Bloch and the other members of the Berkeley Poetry Group; and to Marilyne Bertoncini and Brigitte Gyr for their translations of several poems into French.

Only a garden can teach gardening.

Douglas Dunn

Madame Martin and I

Madame Martin will throw back her shutters at eight
One arm will scoop up sun
She will brush her hair on the stoop using a small pane
        as a mirror
Cap of hair like a well-scoured pot
Bouncing a little
Like the branch the goldfinch just quit.

Monsieur Martin died last summer no
Last last summer
A quiet man
Who liked to do chores round the yard
Spray the roses
Who liked to paint his garden gate green
Every summer
Leafy leafy forest green

She'll rake the gravel – *he* would do that – and pull some weeds
Peg white sheets across the yard
Like a seascape with sails
        across the vanishing point
She'll tie an apron about her waist
Fingers doing that brief couple dance
Over and under and bow to your partner

He was sick all of a sudden
He was dead
And now he's gone
She says she thinks she hardly knew him.

All Souls

They have their backs to the altar
The concert-goers bundled into their overcoats.
They face the music
One freckled fist knuckled on each knee.

Which hand? God asks. *Which hand?*

The Hotel Eden

after Joseph Cornell

Fragments of a life, protected under glass:
A parrot on its perch. A crock of corks. Butt-end of an egg.
The spring from a gutted clock.
This poster for Eden
Scorched and brittle as a boy's treasure map.

On the tip of God's tongue, the bird waits to be named.
Profoundly silent, the taxidermist's shop. 'If only,'
    thinks the bird.
If only what?

Against survival. *Against* feathers. *Against* corks-in-bottles. *Against*
    the pathos of stuffed birds. *Against* against.

From laughter to slaughter the house of objects is repossessed.
The knife recalls the flint flakes.
The flint nodule dreams the chalk cliff.

There's a key to it somewhere. Break the glass?

Landline

He disliked the phone, that hard-shelled crab
Hunkered in the den.
If he had to pick it up he'd say,
'Hello, I'll get your mother,' or
'Your mother's on the other line, goodbye.'
Took me years to notice
We'd never had a conversation on the phone.

Retired now, he fished, gardened, read
Paperbacks borrowed from the library,
The ones that make time go by. He dreamed.
Yes, I think he dreamed. Visiting in summer
I'd catch him, a tool dangling from his hand,
Staring at the mainland across Georgia Strait,
One foot in the sun,
The other in the shade – the watered lawn.
As if he'd forgotten what he came out for.

'What's with the phone?' I asked him.
We were picking oysters. The tide low –
We could walk to the rocky outcrop
We called our 'island.' My imagination's
Prime waterfront, and origin.
Stalking the tide-line, a heron watched us
Warily. I still try to sneak up on them,
You only get so close before they bolt.

He thought for a moment,
Then – half-jokingly – that was his way –
Offering me an oyster
He'd shucked to slurp – replied,
'I guess I'm afraid
That when I pick up there'll be somebody there.'

End of conversation. The tide had turned:
Water was lapping the purple sea stars
Clumped in fissures,
Favelas of mussels and barnacles.
We sloshed back across the shingle
With our bucket of oysters,
The silence not uncomfortable.

A Community Garden

Me pascunt olivae, / me cichorea levesque malvae

We're weeding the raspberry canes
When we notice them – three couples
Snapping selfies, who disappear
Into the rows of corn, and reappear
Later, near us, talking in a language
None of us knows
Although we have several languages between us.
In the background, clucking,
The hens forage and brood.

The youngest couple – diffidently –
Question us,
Translating our answers for their elders,
Grandparents
I'm assuming, round-faced as sunflowers,
Nodding, too, especially
The old man, laugh lines
Converging towards the corners of his eyes,
Serge trousers wrong for here.

California drought. The ground is baked,
Pulling weeds
Without breaking the roots is slow, repetitive work;
Hands grope, minds wander...
It's a recipe for peace – of a sort.

The old man squats down. Soon –
You need to water, he mimes,
Soften the ground. We agree, and go on weeding
With our hands and small tools.
We're water-thrifty, we explain;
The young couple translates. The old man nods
And goes on weeding.
After a while – *You need better tools.*
He stands and makes a foot-on-pitchfork motion,
Squats back down.

His wife and children grow impatient.
He ignores them. He is happy weeding.
We are happy too.
The raspberry canes
Are looking cared for
(A plot of ground is being tended).
Behind, the corn shoots straight up;
Summer squash swell under fat leaves;
The earth is warm, brown.
Later we'll collect the eggs.

The old man stands. He stares
After the rest of his family who are walking off,
Backs turned,
Abandoning him like a stubborn child.
He grins at us and trails
After them for whatever else they've scheduled
This already scorching
August Saturday afternoon.

Olives, Endives and Mallow

after Horace

What does the poet ask of Apollo?
For what does he pray as they pour
The libation from the clay bowl?
Not fertile Sardinia's fields of rich corn,

Nor the herds of sweltering Calabria;
Not the ivory of India
Nor the fecund acres the slow
Liris eats away in its quiet flow.

May those on whom Fortune smiles prune their vines
With high-end Calenian blades;
Let the trader guzzle the wines
He gets in exchange for Syria's goods –

Friended on high, doesn't he go scot-free
In every port, no matter how
Indignant the winds? – As for me,
I feast on olives, endive and mallow.

Grant me, Apollo, calm and contentment,
A healthy body, a mind clear,
And let my old age be spent
Without dishonour nor the sound of my lyre.

The Builders

Clink of a spade chipping dirt.
   Voices of labourers
Sinking posts into wet cement.

Sibilance of aspens rustling.
   Soft-spoken voices speaking
Spanish under soft-spoken aspens.

Shriek of a chainsaw ripping wood.
   Click of an empty stapler.
Shovel thunk against aspen suckers.

Ripples of laughter
   Racing like water
Down a bed of loaf-shaped boulders.

Sound of a gate bolt shot.
   Thud of a tailgate dropped.
Sigh of the gathered up tools.

Roller Skates, a Snack, a Book

I stopped for traffic yesterday
By the entrance to the playground
On the wooded edge of town,
Louis Something's hunting ground,

When a kid flashed though the gate
Down the dirt path with her pup,
Her dad – I guess it was – right
Behind, trying to keep up.

Park and woods are close to school.
I'd go there every week
With roller skates, a snack, a book
To read, the kids of course.

Girl and dad (I guess) trail off –
Not precisely hand in hand –
To the clearing where sandbox,
Seesaws and zip-line stand

Among benches set for parents –
All things I could not have seen
Where I sat, impatiently
Waiting for the stop light to turn green.

Crouching Woman (Camille Claudel)

In old age she thinks it would be good to squat at the side of the road writing in the dust with a stick.

What will she write?

About giving birth. Facing death. Sleeping under the stars, which are very big (and some not there at all any more), and she is small.

A message, say, like the child who finds a piece of driftwood and squatting, heels flat on the ground, centre of gravity close to the sand, prints some words in block letters on the foreshore of a beach. Words only gulls and pelicans can read.

A few lines in the dust. Or the wet sand of a beach before the tide turns. Five, or six lines, say, like a child's drawing of a house.

Monday Morning, Croissy-sur-Seine

Car locks zapped
I exit the underground
Garage, a borrowed mystery
Under my arm.
What am I thinking?
Trying not to think.
Not trying not to think.
Not thinking.
Doing laps in the cool
Pool of myself.

Gut-freezing din.
Shocked, I spin
To the splotch of green
Where the river bends
Past the football pitch
Where a skein of geese
Bursts brush and weeds
And lifts
Like a single mind
To the November sky.

At the delivery dock
A driver offloads pallets
Of drinks: shrink-wrapped
Water bottles, soda
In desire-red cans.
See those geese? he asks,
No sign
Of them now
Though
To riddle our allotment of sky.

Future Perfect

Yesterday he thought *le futur*
Was a tense they taught you in school
Where if you make a mistake
It's not the end of the world.

Well he learned his lesson
God now give him
His book bag back
Let him be on his way home again

No big boys at the construction site
Taking his back pack
His brand new anorak.
And no telling Dad

Who 1) won't go to the cops
For what's just one more case of extortion
Between a boy from Martinique
And some fairer-skinned toughs;

2) Won't go to the construction site
…One brick another brick
Another… till Dad's balled-up on the ground
Like a test you failed

Yesterday – only yesterday
God let him be on his way home again
With a little pocket money
To buy a treat at the bakery.

Hornets

The hornets are polishing off the grapes
That ramble over the south-facing wall.
A season's vine leaves are turning yellow;
The hornets and the hornets' reflections
Plunder the overripe pulp.
What do hornets do with all that nectar?

I sit in a white plastic garden chair.
My coffee mug steams on a boulder.
The leaves cast tremulous shadows.
The hornets shuttle cluster to cluster,
Glide crosswise, down: helicopters –
That's what I think of – the way they hang
Motionless over the clusters,
Pinpoint a target, home in, sidle off.

Collateral Damage

It listed east, liable, the arborist warned, to topple
Into the street, rumple a car,
The neighbours' shipshape house and flint-brick wall,

So Friday, first thing, in hard-hats and gloves,
They fell it – chainsaws wailing – beginning
With the high branches and dream-catcher leaves.

By quitting time the ash tree is strewn
Groin-deep in the yard,
Limbs and brushwood prepped for the mulch machine,

And a rabble of garden birds surveys the debris
Where this morning
Their homely nests and high lookouts had been.

An Ancient Art

To keep the darkness at arm's length
We adorned our walls
With storybook animals stick figures
Brandishing toy weapons

      Images firelight may have lit
      Sequentially
      Producing the illusion of motion

To while away winter evenings
We whittled
From the wing bones of mute swans
Flutes a musician's breath resuscitated

      And Earth Mother
      Humming along stirred her broth
      With a nice clean tibia

Across from the Apple Store

À 115 ans, cette soupe est toujours populaire – Le Parisien

Two hundred servings of Noria's stew –
Still they rattle the lace-curtained door
Negotiating a titbit-to-go –

> *My mate is sick, he can't make it this once,*
> *Will you give me a bite for him?*

No's the response. Come in, drop your bag,
Here's a chair beside Mo with his jar
Of coriander, Pops, his sole flapping,

Or Viktor, the poky eater who rails
If I swab his table –
How can I eat with the smell of bleach?

Faster's the answer. Others are waiting.
Guys with packs big as punching bags
Who say please and thank you as their elders taught them

In Bucharest Bamako Krakków
Men who just lift their bowls
And point to their stomachs. Seconds are allowed.

Gypsies, On the Road

after Baudelaire

Fire-eyed, the fortune-telling tribe left
Last night, they packed up and left, slinging tots
On their backs, offering proud appetites
The ready treasure of a pendulous breast.

Menfolk strapped with gleaming weapons
March by the wagons that hold their families,
Scanning the heavens with smouldering eyes
Heavy with regret for lost illusions.

The cricket, holed up in its sandy den,
Sees them go by and chirps even louder;
Cybele, who loves them, makes the road greener,

Makes the rocks stream and the deserts flower
For these travellers, whose way is open
To the familiar realm of a dim future.

Real Estate

A man with a sensual mouth re-knots
His scarf in the glass of the Shop
Of Ownership Dreams: room upon room
With working fireplaces, and tall windows
To tempt the out-of-doors in and frame it.
His eyes mirror the eyes of the woman
Pony-tailing her hair in an *atelier d'artiste*
And time for a heartbeat stops
Kicking sandwich papers and homeless cans
Around the terrace of the café
Where one might sit and watch
Roma array their wealth of yellow foam
And gaily-flowered bedding
In the capacious shadows of Saint-Sulpice.

In the Luxembourg Garden

An Eternity

They've been here forever, the regulars,
Jaundiced as the little copse of birch trees,
Toasted round the edges like chestnut leaves.

Three-deep they doze over book and fountain,
Haunt the lyric glade where Verlaine glares,
Rent sailboats for blonde cherubim to launch

Or school them in Guignol; on a studious bench
They straddle lovers or slump with heads thrown
Back, feet propped upon an idle chair

And let the sun fondle their flesh.
A finger marks the page, a cuff of cigarette ash
Lengthens until without a sound

It separates, winks in the iron air,
Timeless as cosmic dust confettis down.

Pelouse Interdite

The older man lopes off across the lawn
Trimmed with iron barbed to mimic bramble
And garden chairs painted an indulgent green,
Straight-backed or low-slung and comfortable
To read a book or all the afternoon
Paper in. His wife sings out his name –
He just floats on across the forbidden
Grass, skirting beds of summer bloom,

Until she wades into the pool of green,
And reaching him, tugs on his arm to lead
Him back to the established path. A guardian
Has seen them trespass – they're not unruly –
She whistles at the two students instead,
Over by the beehives playing frisbee.

The Fête du Miel

When summer is over, the beekeepers
Sell their excess honey to the neighbours.

Is it the mythic precincts that gives
Its savour to the honey from these hives?

Or is it the pollution? Wishful thinking
The walls of our Garden. Blackbirds sing,

Bees suck where they will – on dog-pissed street trees
Exhaust-fuelled geraniums and ivies,

As on the blossoms of an apple tree
Coddled by a Carthusian in a monastery.

Last winter was so warm the bees thought
Summer never ended, the beekeepers write

On notices posted round the hives. 'All winter
The bees were out foraging for nectar.

Finding little, they consumed their reserves.
There's no honey to sell this September.'

At the Museum (Fantin-Latour)

A modest age, of buttoned up young men
And girls with strictly-parted hair
Intent on canvases and books. No one
Stares boldly from the picture frame,
The fruit is unambiguously ripe.
In age – in rage? he tried his hand at nudes:
Morning's flamboyant curls and drowsy flesh
Dissolving into sheets of rumpled cloud;
Truth toasted by the poets in top hats.

No risky Odalisque. No erotic
Picnics on the grass. Alas! no undressed
Bourgeois gentlemen discoursing – on what? –
Their penises as silky as cocoons.
His dewy roses are for looking at.

The Queens of France

'Pardon, Madame?' Aggrieved, the tone.
She's cornered an armchair, my neighbour, one
Of the comfy, low-slung ones, unmatched
For reading; and a straight one for her feet.
'Can you stop that?' *Stop rocking on your chair*,
She means, stop rocking like some antsy kid.
'Sorry,' I mutter, returning to *Crossed
Destinies*. Though now I also spy on her.

When clouds frown up our common sun
She folds *Le Monde* just so, stows her pen
And notebook and – what? (she stands) – a cushion
For her bum? In Mylar? In crinkled gold
Mylar engineered for some unearthly cold?
She retreats, I advance and, settling in,
Wait for light's shadows to return and dance
Over the statues of the Queens of France.

In the Orchard

The Luxembourg Palace clock strews its chimes
Over Euclidean parterres, and a sentry
Swivels to ogle a jogger. Seasonal palms
Migrate towards the Orangerie.

Back in the southwest quadrant with the bees,
Stripped heirloom apple and pear trees
(A persimmon still indecent with fruit),
I watch the sun dip behind Montparnasse.
More ripe chestnuts plop into the grass,
The last kids are bribed off the carousel

(Baudelaire aloof on his pedestal),
And my neighbours conclude their lovers' spat –
Chérie, je t'en prie, stop! One cold snap
And the whole baroque décor will collapse.

Défense de Pisser

The boulistes stand in a puddle of sun.
Belotte players pause over a table,
Kibitzers playing a double game. They've
Recycled kitchen chairs – 50s, 60s
Chrome, laminate and vinyl-upholstered
Discards. A remnant of beige broadloom
Dresses the plywood tabletop.

Cabbies off-duty, shopkeepers, pensioners,
This is their club: *L'Amicale
Des Joueurs de Pétanque, Défense de Pisser.*
A snack bar sells beer and shiny helium hearts.

In alcoves, under laurels, lovers smooch,
Diminutive nymphs, elfin boys,
Their soundtracks piping what?
They serenade September's disorder –
Blowsy maples sporting gold ruffs,
Horse chestnuts as lustrous as viols
Casting off their sea-urchin husks.
The players call time-out for a piss
And I, having children to fetch,
Will my steps towards the exit, kicking leaves.

Autumn Song

after Baudelaire

Now we will plunge into the cold shadows;
So long, dancing light of our short summers!
Already I hear the funereal blows
Of firewood ricocheting off the cobbles.

Winter is going to repossess my soul –
Anger, hate, frissons, horror, drudgery,
And like the sun caught in its polar hell
A raw frozen lump's what my heart will be.

I shudder as each log strikes the cobbles;
A gallows' raising would resound the same.
I feel like some tower that collapses
Under the assault of a battering ram.

Lulled by the thuds' monotony, I dream
They nail a coffin together somewhere.
Who for? –Yesterday summer; today autumn!
The mysterious noise rings like departure.

A Stone Bench

'Let's go have a look at those stones' –
I mean the jumble of tombstone-sized slabs
They dug up last spring
When they resurfaced the road past the house
And dumped
Under a mulberry tree outside Paul's chicken run.
I want a bench like his –

A place to sit at the end of the day
And contemplate the Plain,
Roads winding through pine and cypress,
And now
In December
Wisps of smoke rising from outlying farms…
Smoke from Paul's pipe obscuring his face;

Or that's how it used to be: our views
Blocked by a house in what was a wedge
Of olive trees where, one snowbound Christmas,
Paul shot a pheasant
And brought it to us to pluck and roast.

It's still in our heads, and in glimpses from the attic windows.

Paul sits on his retaining wall,
Handsaw dangling.
He's pruning a mulberry tree: the limbs
Heaped to be sawed,
Added to the stacks in his shed.

I run my hands over the stones,
Each rough, each different, calculate the distance
To our front door,
Think of Stonehenge…

'Stay away from the blue stones,'
Paul counsels, 'they crumble.'
But they all look grey to me, pocked, weathered,
Laid – how long ago? – to bridge
The ditch between road and house: brute
As sculptures
Whose forms are still emerging.

A ladder pokes through the tree.
'You ought to be careful,' we say,
'That trunk's rotten, a limb could break.
Maybe yours.'

'It makes shade in summer, I like to park
My car under it.'

'Haven't you got enough wood already?'

Firewood is the last crop.
Pick the cherries, pick the apricots, pick the grapes,
Pick the olives and take them to the mill,
Cut and chop wood.
My brother-in-law says that Paul has wood
For two lifetimes.

'You never know,' Paul says.
On ne sait jamais
One day I might not be able to cut wood.
Then I'll be burning it
Without replacing it. And I might be cold.'

Je pourrais avoir froid...

'If you only burn the wood
From the top of the stacks,' I ask, curious,
'The wood at the bottom
Was cut a long time ago?'

'My father cut the wood
At the bottom of the piles.'
He contemplates his saw,
Adds with a sly smile:

Le vieux pour le vieux.

You Never Know

He's no tourist, Roland swears; it's his wife
Who won't stay put, for her he missed
The hunting season's opening week
For *7 Days 6 Nights in Africa* –

Paul condoles. *He* bagged a hare,
A brace of partridge he plucked and froze –
Freezer and woodpile, they concur,
Backup for a rainy day. *You never know.*

A transplant to their old world,
I soak up their lore, two *paysans* –
Countrymen, and proud,
One unmarried, one whose son
The army has trained to be a doctor.

Roland's eyes shine – a diminutive bird
Lit on their hotel sill.
Hues never dreamed! Not our diminished golds....

Night falls earlier now...

Inside Paul's, a rainbow lights
The head of red-leaf lettuce
The oilcloth-protected supper table.

Four Seasons (a Draft)

Seen close up people's eyes are mere blobs of paint
Step back and they are filled with life
And in some with immanence and imminence of death
Fullness not against but *with* emptiness
The apple on the bough the field of snow.

In Hockney's *Four Seasons,* you see time pass
As each frame of the road merges
Seamlessly into the next loss
Autumn's crisp renunciations spring's silky resurrections
In my gut an ache so sharp I can't stay
I get up
I take the escalator to another level

★

Space and motion only relative – (Leibniz?)
The watch on the wrist of the person
Pacing the deck of the moving ship, shore receding
And so forth
Ad infinitum

★

But, Monet's magpie on a gate whose shadow
Reaches across the field of snow towards us –
But, Chardin's russets glowing
In the pewter bowl *as does eternity...?*

Provisional

Stacked on the sill, gold through
And through, this morning's view –
Six half-pint jars of eucalyptus honey

Friends arrayed last weekend
On a small sidewalk stand
On a bright-red cloth, August's heist of honey;

And the world going by
Stops to talk and to buy
Each a share of the bee colony's bounty,

Quintessence of summer
(Won't last until winter)
Six lucid jars, our provision of honey.

Red Berries

This morning I walked
To the farmer's market
Half a mile over
Half a mile back

I bought two slabs
Of the wild salmon
Sweet butter
To seize it in
A wedge of ripe cheese
('Ready to surrender'
– *Il s'abandonne* –
The goat farmer said)
And a basket
Of the red berries

    Under every message
    Another message

Courtly Love

Who was the poet claimed
Beauty lasts long-
Er in the flesh than in the mind?
He got that wrong

Surely, or why is she
So bothered at the thought
Of those three
Buttons undone at his throat?

They fluster her. Troubadours
Who do not know
Their ladies, they profess,

Know minds have nimble fingers
To undo
The pearly buttons of the flesh.

The Lady and the Hollyhock

Yearly, in September,
Moseying to the gym
I turn at the corner
Bookstore to the museum
Where a courtly Lady
Presides over a Garden
And its bestiary.
It's a pretty vision.

I stick to the courtyard
Where hollyhocks have sprung
From a seam of sand
Unravelled in the paving,
Flower after lusty flower
Blazing against the wall.
They're party-crashing here
Underneath that gargoyle.

A hollyhock's a weed
Good for a kitchen plot,
Guardian of small road
Or vacant, thistled lot,
Somehow someone allows
To prosper in this spot
Underneath a gargoyle
Who's just a water spout.

Exotic Perfume

after Baudelaire

When, with eyes closed on some warm autumn night,
I catch a whiff of your hospitable breast,
I see happier shores go bounding past
Dazzled by the sun's monotonous light;

A leisurely place to which Nature brings
Exotic trees, fruit oozing with flavour,
Men whose lean bodies are full of vigour,
Women whose frank looks are surprising.

Led by your scent towards that blessed isle,
I find harbours bristling with masts and sails
Still tossed by the wind and the waves' rough swell,

And the tamarind perfume that all day long
Hangs in the air, stinging my nostrils,
Blends in my soul with the sailors' song.

Off Frenchman's Road

A surf of white poppies I think I saw once –
Fibrous stems flaunting downy buds
(Jiggling scrotums of secret flounce),
With petals pleated, puckered, crumpled, crushed,
The stamens' daunting jubilant yellow
Wooing the pistil's seed-jammed case.
A froth of white poppies, occupying the place!

I grabbed a bunch to stuff in a glass,
Put it where the light would shine through them
Conflating their shadow
With my spoons and pots – till tomorrow
Dusted my kitchen's milky laminate
With day-glo pollen and the flotsam
Of linen-white petals shed in the night.

Aubade for a House Exchange, Summer 2003

Feeling right at home here in Palo Alto
Under the roses that trellis your patio,

> Anti-war posters on Eric's van
> Squatting the drive like a jaded Buddha.

Through your good-neighbour fence I spy Jan
Hanging out wash, white & straight as America's teeth.

> God Bless Towels and Sheets!

Sexy, the fuchsia that jiggles its hips
At the backyard's maidenhair ferns. No squirrels yet...

> We're still on Paris time –
> Jet lag is why we're up at *this ungodly hour,*

As my mother would say. Summers she skipped church.
Family custom she swore that Sunday (morning, her time)

> I called and caught her
> In the garden, glorifying roses.

Moon with a Supermarket Trolley

From my Juliet balcony
Overlooking a creek whose bed
Has been trash-filled for months,
Moon, I see you preening like a supermodel –

Nothing to do with me, or any
Of those other heavenly bodies
So difficult to discern
Through the excess of human light –

But what on earth is that supermarket trolley
Abandoned in the thatch
On your parched banks?
Listen! Even the crickets tsk-tsk.

Herbarium

A walled garden with a low door
Up to the café-cum-grocery-
    P.O. and church,
Down to the brook and cemetery;

In the middle a mulberry tree
Offers shade from the summer heat,
    A clothesline moored
To its scarred grey trunk. And a white

Table rusting in the gravel,
    With three slatted
Chairs, two of them broken, all
Needing paint. Everything is old

And serviceable; that sheet drying
On the line was stitched together
    From two of a great aunt's ones, worn
Thin in the centre.

Take that says the hunter's shotgun
From vineyards ripe for harvesting.
    Buzz of a chainsaw –
Someone else repairing something.

Life

Going on 97 now. Or is it 98?
Most of your moving parts have seized up
Like that Beetle we let rust in the drive –
Glad when they towed it away.
    Six o'clock. Suppertime. The girl brings a tray.
Here is a table, here is a chair, here
Is a soup spoon we lay in your hand,
Watch you try to find your mouth. This is life?
    Well, as you said last week
After your winning streak at dominoes,
Perhaps The Good Lord is punishing you
For your attempted escape, two, three years ago
(Why are we so vague?)
When they caught you in the act
And dragged you back to do the rest of your time.

On The Existence of Doubt

If she entertained any doubts
About the meaning of life the old woman
Kept them to herself, like china she trusted
No one to wash.
Once she mentioned a feeling of unworthiness.
Once she expressed regret for some impatience.

When she was a girl on the Prairies
The winters were longer
But the skies were bigger
And there were no coastal mountains to hem you in
And no coast

Why must we relinquish these things –
Children untarnished in their frames, the tobacco pot
Smelling of Father's pipe, rhubarb's
Great fleshy ears
Funneling rain back into the earth?

Once, long ago, when they were tidying
The grass around her own mother's stone,
Her child enquired about her Faith
In God and Heaven and Meeting Again.
The Old Rugged Cross, wasn't that the hymn?

Children should not ask questions.

For Now

On my desktop I've saved the photograph.
Her at the kitchen table
In the last house but one.

In no time she'll be backing out –
Juice oranges, bacon, eggs,
Top up gas (PetroCanada down a cent) –

But for now she consents to sit
And her dressing gown's carnation pink
Is set off by the periwinkle

Blue jug of milk; against her breast she cradles
The new child
And behind through unrained-on glass

Blissfully climbing to the August sky
Are the pinprick
Lights of a stalk of rue.

Old Women

after Baudelaire

In the winding folds of old capitals
Where all, horror, even, is enchanting,
I – alert to the inevitable –
Spy some beings, decrepit and charming.

Monstrosities, once young and beautiful –
Éponine…Laïs! We love their humped backs
And twisted limbs! Monsters, they are souls still.
Under holey skirts and skimpy fabrics

They creep, whipped by the north wind's spiteful clacks,
Startled by the roar of some omnibus,
Clutching to their sides, like precious relics,
A purse stitched with flowers or a rebus;

They drag themselves like wounded animals,
They lurch and totter like marionettes.
Or they dance without meaning to, poor bells
A heartless demon tugs on. They are wrecks,

But their eyes, that are sharp as gimlets still,
Shine like the holes water sleeps in at night;
Their eyes are the eyes of the little girl
Who laughs in wonder at everything bright.

★

I've watched so many of these old women!
One, one late afternoon when sunset streaked
The sky with a bloody vermillion,
Sat on a bench, alone, lost in thought,

For one of those band concerts rich in brass,
With which soldiers are wont to flood our parks,
And which, on gold evenings that revive us,
Spark heroism in civilian hearts.

This woman, proud, spine ramrod straight,
Eyes widening at times like an old eagle's,
Was soaking up the vital warrior beat;
Her marble brow looked fit for laurels.

A Happy Ending

It is Christmas Day evening in our village – my husband's village – in Provence. One of the cousins remembers a story, old doings still present in her mind. *Stop me if you've heard it before.*

Story-telling is an art in Provence. Everyone has a fund of tales. The pauses, the winks, the *sotto voce*, the gestures, the audience as claque and chorus. But last winter our cousin tripped and fell; now sometimes she's fine, others she forgets who is alive, who has died, what happened to this one, what to another. Her husband is worried. Suppose she muddles the storyline? Maybe he should tell the story? She gives him a scornful look…

> *It was noon; we'd just arrived in the village and I was hurrying across the square to the grocery shop. Victorine, who is leaning as usual on the parapet of her terrace, calls down to me:*
>
> *So, you've come to stay for a while?*
>
> *Yes, but I have to get to the shop before it closes, I'll stop on my way back.*

★

Careful, M's husband warns, and he also points out that her stocking has wrinkled down. She pulls it up.

★

> *There was only one customer in the shop. She wasn't from here. Pierrette was putting her purchases into her basket, one, two, three, four, five tomatoes, and then – hup! – she glances at me over the other woman's head and shrugs, as if to say, I have to get rid of this one too – and she adds the sixth tomato, which is rotten, and the customer who isn't from here says thank you and goes out.*

Pierrette looks at me, excited. The mayor's wife died!

What happened?

She ate and she ate and she ate, and she swelled and she swelled and she swelled, and then she died.

I go back across the square with my basket of groceries. Victorine is still leaning with her arms folded on the parapet of her terrace waiting for me.

Did you hear? she asks.

About the mayor's wife? Yes, what happened?

She ate and she ate and she ate, and she wasted and she wasted and she wasted, and then she died.

★

Brava! M's husband cries. Brava – ! He is glad. She remembered all the story's details in the correct order.

We are all glad. We are picking at the Christmas leftovers in our cousins' house. The storytellers are telling their stories, the same events in the same order with the same happy endings. Nothing has changed.

Happy he who like Ulysses

after du Bellay

Happy he who like Ulysses has made
A fine voyage, or won the Golden Fleece,
And returned, full of wisdom and sense,
To live with his kin the rest of his days.

When will I see again my little village
Chimney smoking, and in what season
The hedges around my modest cottage,
Which is my province and my heart's reason?

I prefer the house my ancestors built
To a Roman palace's grand fronton,
Better than hard marble I like thin slate:

My Gallic Loire over Tiber's Latin,
My little Liré over Palatine,
Better than sea air, the mild Angevine.

Winter Pears

On the road that descends into La Roque,
After the picnic table
And high-perched cemetery, a pear tree gnarls
Up from a farmyard, hoarding its pears.
A sin to let these fat pears go to waste,
This abundance my fingers ache to pick
(Rotting fruit already litters the ground):
I knock at the farmhouse and ask,
Do they belong to the pears and may we pick some?

But the woman drying her hands on a tea towel
Smiles no, not her pears,
They belong – she points farther down –
The house we stopped at yesterday to read
The handwritten warning tacked to the gate

> *mon chien court les 200m en 10 secondes*
> *si tu cours moins vite*
> *restes au portail et sonnes!*

> my dog covers 200m in 10 seconds
> if you don't run that fast
> stay at the gate and ring!

We ring, the dog comes belting,
I snatch my hand back
And wait for the lady of the house
In plaid felt slippers
Who is just fine with us picking some pears.

Don't you eat them? I ask.
A few, she hedges,
Adding, *They're winter pears, they're hard,*
Good only for cooking.

This morning, breakfast done, I lift the pears
From the top of the fridge, and I sort them –
The unblemished
And the windfalls. I take the black-handled,
Paper-thin knife that has been in the kitchen
For maybe a hundred years
The knife that brings to my mind
The black-handled knives that Chardin
Places slantwise across his surfaces,
Utensils
That give his paintings their illusion of depth;

And I carve out the bruises, the fine-bore
Tunnels of worms.
I slice the fruit thinly, until the white flesh
Is almost translucent,
I arrange the slices in the new pot from Ikea
        (I burned the old one),
Add a trickle of water
And leave them to simmer.

Three Fragments

The third is a woman's head.
She is watching the bread rise.
The loaves sit on the yellow-tiled counter
Below the stopped clock.
Her head fills with the smell of yeast.

★

Periwinkle blue the sun
Behind the church. And gold to the east where chestnut leaves
Flicker down, toss, curl
In gutters. Soon the teams
Of sweepers, the chorus of brooms.

★

Blue says Tragedy. Red replies Comedy.
The argument continues into the night.

Many Moons

A mystery why that plus-size moon
Bobbing in the front window
Disappears if I tilt to the left

      – a trick I repeat like the child
      who throws
      a toy from his crib and reels it back in –

      gone back   gone back

Till it dawns on me that that mother of a moon
Stealing the show
From planes stacked to land at SFO,

A planet or two, and a raft of stars
That for all I know
Are just the after-glow
      of their long-extinguished selves,

Is merely a reflection of the one
Just now
Sailing free of the redwood trees in the window
      behind me.

Behind

Javier Garcerà, Madrid

Your new canvas was a honeycomb
Of windows through the fretwork leaves,
Panes too far or too small to see in.

I am interested in what behind *means*,
You said. Which was all you'd say.
Tracery leaves, lit panes and a sunset-

Through-pollution bleed: overlaid planes
Of the perceptible
Before the voracious mind barges in

Waking meaning's echo chamber.
From your studio wall a mirror
Looked back at us, and at you *behind*,

Dousing the spoon-bright anchovies
In olive oil,
Uncorking the slatey Portuguese wine.

The Sand Dollar Inn

Ocean Views from Every Room

Here, engraved in someone else's
Name, is a bench where we can sit
And watch the waves go in and out.
Lean back, sop up the horizontal sun
Trawling west across the Strait.
Why don't I leave you here?
Why don't I take a stroll out where
The tide will turn, that wave-stamped
Strand of wetter, darker sand
Where families shore up their castle walls
And sift debris for intact shells
Faux gems of bottle glass and fossil scraps
Of runic, worm-written wood
The sea collects for us to hold.

The First Memory

In a forties Chevrolet
We move from English Bay
To a stucco bungalow
Three will unpack now
Near a park – scrap wilderness –
Whose old-growth trees
Are lightning-charred
Where one polio summer
A boy will hold me
Underwater
The time it takes to burn
A memory. I will return
To English Bay with Dad,
This quiet man
Who sits in the kitchen
At 3 a.m. drinking Bovril.
I made myself a cup of Bovril,
He says and I reply
It's cold in the spare room.

Moving Day, the Chevy:
The first memory.
The one in which Dad stepped
From the ranks of returned
Soldiers
And hurried shyly towards us
Is missing
From the place memories are.

Lost and Found

When a text was no longer read
Its oak-gall ink could be scraped off,
The parchment recycled,
In which case the first text was usually lost;

    Or scrubbed with milk and oat bran.
    In that case the first text might reappear
    A ghostly *scriptio inferior* –
    Object's memory, ingrained.

So Archimedes' palimpsest
Comes to light, underwriting Christian prayers,
And memories we think or fear or hope are lost
May lie dormant for years,

    Till, jostled by some scent or taste,
    They claim a new lease on life
    And swell the restless host
    That cross-examines me at night.

On the Naming of Hurricanes

Dido. Cleo. Gloria. Katrina.
A force of nature? Unpredictable,
Violent, devastating –
A name for shelter swept away?

Men did the naming, naturally. Still
Wouldn't you think they'd name
A work of theirs – wee skirmish even – after themselves?
Marathon. Agincourt. Verdun.

Dad went to war. Returned
With a drab canteen, printed
With his name and rank. *Good box,* says my son.
Good for keeping stuff in.
Dad was pretty taciturn.

I stored it in the basement,
My go-to when I'm afraid
I'm going to hurt my squabbling kids.
Small as a darning egg
I watch the furnace lick its flames.

Take it, I tell my boy. *Take Dad's army box.*
Use it as you please. But please
Steer clear of Mother's rage
And the battles no general wants to name.

After the Quake

I saved this photo
From the *Times*: Sichuan, 2008,
A squandered

Child, cheek
Nestled in her father's clavicle.
Jittery as wrens

The father's eyes
Record the aftershocks
Paper can't contain.

Dust films her pullover,
The fuzzy one she wore
To school today. Today?

Today's this egg
Snug in her palm,
Round and precarious as a belly

Full of child.
Was the egg pulled
From the rubble too?

She's holding it – for now
She's rescued
And will keep it safe.

Letter Home

from a Canadian Stretcher Bearer, 1916

'I want to get a job as Battn stretcher bearer.
It's a rotten job, of course, no one wants it,
But I think I'd be more use binding up wounds
Than just carrying a gun in the ordinary way.

'There's no honour in the damn job, no chance
Of advancement. But I like the work,
And understand it a little, while I hate
Looking after a beastly gun and forming fours and all that.'

States of Siege

For his father Hamoudi cooks soup from grass.
The shepherd tells him what kind the sheep like.

When they killed the donkey I took a few ounces
Though Islam forbids it. Starvation is infidel.

When neighbours slaughter the last horse in town
Ahmed says *I knew that horse.*

★

What poetry matches a litany of facts?

> *another three soldiers and an Afghan*
> *interpreter killed in two blasts* – Globe & Mail

> *sacked houses and temples, they killed*
> *women and infants along with the livestock* – Thucydides

Just give us the facts
In their armoured personnel carriers.

Long House

Or consider the Haida with their hundred-odd words for rain
Their long houses their bald eagles their abalone jewellery
And their elaborate gift-giving economy
That failed to save them from the Europeans
Who wanted their fish their forests and their flags over everything.

H. Erectus

They gasp
To see her stand
No hands
For the first time
In history, clap
For joy: *Bravo!*
Bravo! But o –
They clap hands
To their mouths
Now she wobbles
On the brink
Their small shadow
Break-dancing
With the world
Then falls
Thank god
To all fours again
And the moment that expanded
Shrinks.

First Snow

1

Tonight at dusk as hills
Shy off and the flakes

Start to whirl
We see our boundaries fade

With a sharper sense
Of the unknown. Something

Blurry crosses our field
Of vision

And enters the stand of trees,
Aspen and wild

Animal lope
And the cold that draws

Its cave of memory
Like a skin around us.

2

And what to say
About this mountain ash along the drive
Whose red berries
Are sugar-glazed in frost

And hang
Stunned into silence
In a ruff of
Brown paper leaf?

3
Our boots tromp a path
Through silence
Three magpies watch, one

From the tip of each spruce
Buffered in snow. Magpies –

Mechanical birds,
Three tin cut-outs
Like weather vanes

On a trio of spruce.
Dapper in starched shirts

And metallic blue tails
They natter at us
At us or the dogs

Or the untidy world at large.

4
A patch of ice
Shines between house and house

We go out.
Polar light over glacial hills.
The top rail of the new fence glitters.

Snow has erased each accident.
No need

To apologise now
Small creature that ventured forth
Before dawn

And left us
The small print of your tracks.

Answering Machine

for Chana Bloch

We talked on the phone yesterday,
You in Berkeley, me
In the South Bay, always the bridges
Between us.

Women's conversations.
Benjamin engaged to be married.
They went to Vietnam
To see her mother who won't come –
Too many time zones for an old woman.

The poetry group convened on Sunday.
Sorry I couldn't be there,
I said, we had a wedding – friends
Who've been together for twenty years.
Christophe in fuschia
Socks and a lavaliere,
James more sedate.
Now they get health care in three countries.

You and Dave are off
To L.A. on Monday
To get your results. It's funny,
You said, how happy I feel –
One day at a time

Or it might be the effect of the pills.

★

All winter I've been listening to you
Repeat *I can't come to the phone right now*
I can't come to the phone…
And leaving a message on your machine.

But today when I call
To say I'm driving over to Berkeley
Sunday and I'm thinking
I could drop off
One of my famous Tartes Tatin
Which won't be hot but should still taste good –
And I'll ring the doorbell
And run away like some bad-joke kid

The machine picks up
In someone else's voice.

Land's End

The bridal parties file across the lawn
In too high heels and flimsy dresses,
Boys in rented tuxes
Holding boutonnières in boxes
Like pastries
Or eggs.

Vita brevis days are long.
We sniff the grass that smells
Fresh cut, watch the brides'
Stiletto heels stab porous turf.
The spires of the Golden Gate
Rise through a frieze
Of cypress trees;
The ocean makes a muted din.

Reclining on the grass we watch
Musicians tote
The strange shapes of their instruments
Up the colonnade
To the museum, a replica
Of a replica, whose original –
If one may speak of origins? –

Is in Paris. The bridal parties
Are replicas of something too.
It's all as old as war
And trade murmur the figures

On the bas relief.
We Create Paradise
Replies the purveyor of palms in pots
On every side
Of his immaculate white van.

The sun posts west
But yachts still venture out to sea
And at intervals the foghorns low
Although today
Although today
Although today
There is no fog

The light is consecrating everything.

Scope

for Lucie

Standing on your porch at dusk
We observe the fingernail
Clipping of a moon as it descends
To the opposite ridge

Where a herd of elk – cows and calves –
Also comes to rest
Each day at dusk.
I've never viewed the moon

Through a telescope before:
Tiny craters inside big ones
As if it were scarred
By a childhood disease;

But it's the inner edge
My eye keeps turning to – not the clean-
Swept moon that shines over
Your child's picture-book house,

But ragged, frayed
Like a scrap of lace
That comes to light
From the chaos of a dresser drawer.

The Back Road

We can make a loop.
No need to retrace our footsteps
Strangers tell us
Over the asphalt road that winds
Through vineyards
Back to our own perched village –
There's a path through the woods
Aromatic pine and oak
On the north-facing slope –
And surely circling back
Is better than
Returning over the same ground?

Today we scout the trailhead
Where they said
Under the hill cemetery –
All we find's a road
Downhill into shade and mud
Not up
To *the panoramic view,*
And a signpost inscribed *Chemin de l'Envers –*
Road of the Other Side
Or maybe *Back Road?*

Looks gloomy.
Shouldn't have mooned round the garden
Sipping coffee while wasps laid their eggs
In our figs.
But hey, let's give it a try.

Down we go, into shade.
The road forks, it forks again,
We have choices to make,
But – long story short –
In no time we find our way

Right back to our usual road
Beside a slope of gently blazing vineyards
Where *grappillons* still hang –

Grapes for the gleaners.